My profile

Name : _____

Phone : _____

E-mail : _____

Month	Income	Expense	Saving	Balance
January				
February				
March				
April				
May				
June				
July				
August				
September				
October				
November				
December				
Total				

Result :

Are you satisfied with your financial account?

O Great   O Moderate   O Bad

365 DAYS TO WEALTHY

D/M/Y	ITEMS	INCOME	EXPENSES	BALANCE

D/M/Y	ITEMS	INCOME	EXPENSES	BALANCE

365 DAYS TO WEALTHY

D/M/Y	ITEMS	INCOME	EXPENSES	BALANCE

D/M/Y	ITEMS	INCOME	EXPENSES	BALANCE

365 DAYS TO WEALTHY

D/M/Y	ITEMS	INCOME	EXPENSES	BALANCE

D/M/Y	ITEMS	INCOME	EXPENSES	BALANCE

D/M/Y	ITEMS	INCOME	EXPENSES	BALANCE

D/M/Y	ITEMS	INCOME	EXPENSES	BALANCE

365 DAYS TO WEALTHY

D/M/Y	ITEMS	INCOME	EXPENSES	BALANCE

365 DAYS TO WEALTHY

D/M/Y	ITEMS	INCOME	EXPENSES	BALANCE

365 DAYS TO WEALTHY

D/M/Y	ITEMS	INCOME	EXPENSES	BALANCE

365 DAYS TO WEALTHY

D/M/Y	ITEMS	INCOME	EXPENSES	BALANCE

D/M/Y	ITEMS	INCOME	EXPENSES	BALANCE

365 DAYS TO WEALTHY

D/M/Y	ITEMS	INCOME	EXPENSES	BALANCE

D/M/Y	ITEMS	INCOME	EXPENSES	BALANCE

365 DAYS TO WEALTHY

D/M/Y	ITEMS	INCOME	EXPENSES	BALANCE

D/M/Y	ITEMS	INCOME	EXPENSES	BALANCE

365 DAYS TO WEALTHY

D/M/Y	ITEMS	INCOME	EXPENSES	BALANCE

365 DAYS TO WEALTHY

D/M/Y	ITEMS	INCOME	EXPENSES	BALANCE

365 DAYS TO WEALTHY

D/M/Y	ITEMS	INCOME	EXPENSES	BALANCE

D/M/Y	ITEMS	INCOME	EXPENSES	BALANCE

D/M/Y	ITEMS	INCOME	EXPENSES	BALANCE

365 DAYS TO WEALTHY

D/M/Y	ITEMS	INCOME	EXPENSES	BALANCE

365 DAYS TO WEALTHY

D/M/Y	ITEMS	INCOME	EXPENSES	BALANCE

365 DAYS TO WEALTHY

D/M/Y	ITEMS	INCOME	EXPENSES	BALANCE

365 DAYS TO WEALTHY

D/M/Y	ITEMS	INCOME	EXPENSES	BALANCE

365 DAYS TO WEALTHY

D/M/Y	ITEMS	INCOME	EXPENSES	BALANCE

D/M/Y	ITEMS	INCOME	EXPENSES	BALANCE

D/M/Y	ITEMS	INCOME	EXPENSES	BALANCE

365 DAYS TO WEALTHY

D/M/Y	ITEMS	INCOME	EXPENSES	BALANCE

365 DAYS TO WEALTHY

D/M/Y	ITEMS	INCOME	EXPENSES	BALANCE

D/M/Y	ITEMS	INCOME	EXPENSES	BALANCE

D/M/Y	ITEMS	INCOME	EXPENSES	BALANCE

D/M/Y	ITEMS	INCOME	EXPENSES	BALANCE

D/M/Y	ITEMS	INCOME	EXPENSES	BALANCE

365 DAYS TO WEALTHY

D/M/Y	ITEMS	INCOME	EXPENSES	BALANCE

D/M/Y	ITEMS	INCOME	EXPENSES	BALANCE

D/M/Y	ITEMS	INCOME	EXPENSES	BALANCE

D/M/Y	ITEMS	INCOME	EXPENSES	BALANCE

365 DAYS TO WEALTHY

D/M/Y	ITEMS	INCOME	EXPENSES	BALANCE

365 DAYS TO WEALTHY

D/M/Y	ITEMS	INCOME	EXPENSES	BALANCE

365 DAYS TO WEALTHY

D/M/Y	ITEMS	INCOME	EXPENSES	BALANCE

365 DAYS TO WEALTHY

D/M/Y	ITEMS	INCOME	EXPENSES	BALANCE

D/M/Y	ITEMS	INCOME	EXPENSES	BALANCE

365 DAYS TO WEALTHY

D/M/Y	ITEMS	INCOME	EXPENSES	BALANCE

365 DAYS TO WEALTHY

D/M/Y	ITEMS	INCOME	EXPENSES	BALANCE

365 DAYS TO WEALTHY

D/M/Y	ITEMS	INCOME	EXPENSES	BALANCE

365 DAYS TO WEALTHY

D/M/Y	ITEMS	INCOME	EXPENSES	BALANCE

365 DAYS TO WEALTHY

D/M/Y	ITEMS	INCOME	EXPENSES	BALANCE

365 DAYS TO WEALTHY

D/M/Y	ITEMS	INCOME	EXPENSES	BALANCE

365 DAYS TO WEALTHY

D/M/Y	ITEMS	INCOME	EXPENSES	BALANCE

365 DAYS TO WEALTHY

D/M/Y	ITEMS	INCOME	EXPENSES	BALANCE

D/M/Y	ITEMS	INCOME	EXPENSES	BALANCE

365 DAYS TO WEALTHY

D/M/Y	ITEMS	INCOME	EXPENSES	BALANCE

D/M/Y	ITEMS	INCOME	EXPENSES	BALANCE

D/M/Y	ITEMS	INCOME	EXPENSES	BALANCE

D/M/Y	ITEMS	INCOME	EXPENSES	BALANCE

365 DAYS TO WEALTHY

D/M/Y	ITEMS	INCOME	EXPENSES	BALANCE

D/M/Y	ITEMS	INCOME	EXPENSES	BALANCE

365 DAYS TO WEALTHY

D/M/Y	ITEMS	INCOME	EXPENSES	BALANCE

365 DAYS TO WEALTHY

D/M/Y	ITEMS	INCOME	EXPENSES	BALANCE

365 DAYS TO WEALTHY

D/M/Y	ITEMS	INCOME	EXPENSES	BALANCE

365 DAYS TO WEALTHY

D/M/Y	ITEMS	INCOME	EXPENSES	BALANCE

365 DAYS TO WEALTHY

D/M/Y	ITEMS	INCOME	EXPENSES	BALANCE

365 DAYS TO WEALTHY

D/M/Y	ITEMS	INCOME	EXPENSES	BALANCE

D/M/Y	ITEMS	INCOME	EXPENSES	BALANCE

365 DAYS TO WEALTHY

D/M/Y	ITEMS	INCOME	EXPENSES	BALANCE

D/M/Y	ITEMS	INCOME	EXPENSES	BALANCE

365 DAYS TO WEALTHY

D/M/Y	ITEMS	INCOME	EXPENSES	BALANCE

D/M/Y	ITEMS	INCOME	EXPENSES	BALANCE

D/M/Y	ITEMS	INCOME	EXPENSES	BALANCE

365 DAYS TO WEALTHY

D/M/Y	ITEMS	INCOME	EXPENSES	BALANCE

D/M/Y	ITEMS	INCOME	EXPENSES	BALANCE

D/M/Y	ITEMS	INCOME	EXPENSES	BALANCE

D/M/Y	ITEMS	INCOME	EXPENSES	BALANCE

365 DAYS TO WEALTHY

D/M/Y	ITEMS	INCOME	EXPENSES	BALANCE

365 DAYS TO WEALTHY

D/M/Y	ITEMS	INCOME	EXPENSES	BALANCE

365 DAYS TO WEALTHY

D/M/Y	ITEMS	INCOME	EXPENSES	BALANCE

D/M/Y	ITEMS	INCOME	EXPENSES	BALANCE

365 DAYS TO WEALTHY

D/M/Y	ITEMS	INCOME	EXPENSES	BALANCE

D/M/Y	ITEMS	INCOME	EXPENSES	BALANCE

365 DAYS TO WEALTHY

D/M/Y	ITEMS	INCOME	EXPENSES	BALANCE

D/M/Y	ITEMS	INCOME	EXPENSES	BALANCE

D/M/Y	ITEMS	INCOME	EXPENSES	BALANCE

365 DAYS TO WEALTHY

D/M/Y	ITEMS	INCOME	EXPENSES	BALANCE

D/M/Y	ITEMS	INCOME	EXPENSES	BALANCE

365 DAYS TO WEALTHY

D/M/Y	ITEMS	INCOME	EXPENSES	BALANCE

D/M/Y	ITEMS	INCOME	EXPENSES	BALANCE

365 DAYS TO WEALTHY

D/M/Y	ITEMS	INCOME	EXPENSES	BALANCE

365 DAYS TO WEALTHY

D/M/Y	ITEMS	INCOME	EXPENSES	BALANCE

365 DAYS TO WEALTHY

D/M/Y	ITEMS	INCOME	EXPENSES	BALANCE

365 DAYS TO WEALTHY

D/M/Y	ITEMS	INCOME	EXPENSES	BALANCE

365 DAYS TO WEALTHY

D/M/Y	ITEMS	INCOME	EXPENSES	BALANCE

365 DAYS TO WEALTHY

D/M/Y	ITEMS	INCOME	EXPENSES	BALANCE

D/M/Y	ITEMS	INCOME	EXPENSES	BALANCE

365 DAYS TO WEALTHY

D/M/Y	ITEMS	INCOME	EXPENSES	BALANCE

D/M/Y	ITEMS	INCOME	EXPENSES	BALANCE

365 DAYS TO WEALTHY

D/M/Y	ITEMS	INCOME	EXPENSES	BALANCE

365 DAYS TO WEALTHY

D/M/Y	ITEMS	INCOME	EXPENSES	BALANCE

365 DAYS TO WEALTHY

D/M/Y	ITEMS	INCOME	EXPENSES	BALANCE

D/M/Y	ITEMS	INCOME	EXPENSES	BALANCE

365 DAYS TO WEALTHY

D/M/Y	ITEMS	INCOME	EXPENSES	BALANCE

365 DAYS TO WEALTHY

D/M/Y	ITEMS	INCOME	EXPENSES	BALANCE

365 DAYS TO WEALTHY

D/M/Y	ITEMS	INCOME	EXPENSES	BALANCE

365 DAYS TO WEALTHY

D/M/Y	ITEMS	INCOME	EXPENSES	BALANCE

365 DAYS TO WEALTHY

D/M/Y	ITEMS	INCOME	EXPENSES	BALANCE

365 DAYS TO WEALTHY

D/M/Y	ITEMS	INCOME	EXPENSES	BALANCE

365 DAYS TO WEALTHY

D/M/Y	ITEMS	INCOME	EXPENSES	BALANCE

D/M/Y	ITEMS	INCOME	EXPENSES	BALANCE

365 DAYS TO WEALTHY

D/M/Y	ITEMS	INCOME	EXPENSES	BALANCE

365 DAYS TO WEALTHY

D/M/Y	ITEMS	INCOME	EXPENSES	BALANCE

365 DAYS TO WEALTHY

D/M/Y	ITEMS	INCOME	EXPENSES	BALANCE

D/M/Y	ITEMS	INCOME	EXPENSES	BALANCE

365 DAYS TO WEALTHY

D/M/Y	ITEMS	INCOME	EXPENSES	BALANCE

365 DAYS TO WEALTHY

D/M/Y	ITEMS	INCOME	EXPENSES	BALANCE

D/M/Y	ITEMS	INCOME	EXPENSES	BALANCE

365 DAYS TO WEALTHY

D/M/Y	ITEMS	INCOME	EXPENSES	BALANCE

365 DAYS TO WEALTHY

D/M/Y	ITEMS	INCOME	EXPENSES	BALANCE

365 DAYS TO WEALTHY

D/M/Y	ITEMS	INCOME	EXPENSES	BALANCE

365 DAYS TO WEALTHY

D/M/Y	ITEMS	INCOME	EXPENSES	BALANCE

365 DAYS TO WEALTHY

D/M/Y	ITEMS	INCOME	EXPENSES	BALANCE

365 DAYS TO WEALTHY

D/M/Y	ITEMS	INCOME	EXPENSES	BALANCE

D/M/Y	ITEMS	INCOME	EXPENSES	BALANCE

365 DAYS TO WEALTHY

D/M/Y	ITEMS	INCOME	EXPENSES	BALANCE

D/M/Y	ITEMS	INCOME	EXPENSES	BALANCE

365 DAYS TO WEALTHY

www.ingramcontent.com/pod-product-compliance
Lightning Source LLC
Chambersburg PA
CBHW072210170526
45158CB00002BA/537